A Mennonite in Khiva

A Mennonite in Khiva

Other Titles by the Author

Death is Also Blue (poems in Persian), 2002
The Blue Yarn (poems in Persian), 2009
Awkwardly Do I Walk, 2012
Orange, the Color of Happiness (poems in Persian), 2014
Deer and the Shrines (poems in Persian), 2021

A Mennonite in Khiva

Collected Poems

by

Soheila Amirsoleimani

Ibex Publishers,
Bethesda, Maryland

A Mennonite in Khiva
Poems by Soheila Amirsoleimani

Copyright © 2021 Soheila Amirsoleimani

ISBN: 978-1-58814-142-2

Manufactured in the United States of America

The paper used in this book meets the minimum requirements of the American National Standard for Information Services—Permanence of Paper for Printed Library Materials, ANSI Z39.48–1984

Ibex Publishers strives to create books which are complete and free of error. Please help us with future editions by reporting any errors or suggestions for improvement to the address below or: corrections@ibexpub.com

Ibex Publishers, Inc.
Post Office Box 30087
Bethesda, Maryland 20824
Telephone: 301–718–8188
www.ibexpublishers.com

Library of Congress Cataloging-in-Publication Data

Names: Ameir'sulaymeanei, Suhaylea, author.
Title: A Mennonite in Khiva : poems / by Soheila Amirsoleimani.
Description: First edition. | Bethesda, Maryland : Ibex Publishers, [2017]
Identifiers: LCCN 2016041278 (print) | LCCN 2016048571 (ebook) | ISBN 9781588141422 (alk. paper) | ISBN 9781588141446 (ebook)
Classification: LCC PS3601.M57 A6 2017 (print) | LCC PS3601.M57 (ebook) | DDC 811/.6—dc23

Contents

On a *Mennonite in Khiva*

The story of the lead poem in this collection, "a Mennonite in Khiva," goes back to the summer of 2000 when I visited Khiva, Uzbekistan with Peace Corps volunteers, including my then friend and now husband.

I stayed at a caravanserai in Khiva. When we were having dinner at the caravanserai the very first night, I noticed a group of Mennonite men. The next morning, I woke up very early—almost at dawn. I dressed and left my room. I ended up sitting on the bench in front of my caravanserai, looking at the sun rising and at the mud bricks when out came a Mennonite man whose hat was taking flight in the wind and he was fast running after it. He caught it.

That evening we had dinner with a few friends of the Peace Corps group. Among them was a young man from AmeriCorps, and at some point, he and I realized that we had both witnessed the early morning scene of the hat taking flight and the Mennonite man chasing after it.

The scene and the retelling of it, or the sharing of it with the young man, felt almost like a transcendent moment—one which I carried with me for years. I knew it would stay with me and it has.

A few months ago, a Mennonite gentleman named, Mr. Harold Miller, wrote me, inquiring about this book, containing as it does the word,

"Mennonite." And now meeting him because of the experience in Khiva has sweetened the memory of that day even further.

—Soheila Amirsoleimani,
Salt Lake City, July 25, 2017

A Mennonite in Khiva

a Mennonite in Khiva

Khiva
in
the
early
morning
hours
of
a
summer
day

sitting
on
the
mudbrick
bench
of
the
caravanserai

the sky
slowly
brightening

the
mudbricks

the
sight
of
a Mennonite
man
chasing
down
his
hat
that
blows
away
in the
wind

amazement
and
wonder

shackles of thought

I
want
to
get rid
of
the
shackles
of
thought
and
walk
down
this
long
road
lined
with trees,
their
yellow
orange
and
red leaves
falling
on the
ground.

Friday,
November 2, 2012
Salt Lake City, Utah

old ideas

I live
at
a
point
in time
when
old ideas
about
what
it
means
to live
a good
life
are
at odds
with
the
very
survival
of the
planet—
people
still
grasping
at straws
to
keep
the old

familiar
ways—
fearful
of
what is
yet
to come.

to the memory of
Roslyn Zinn

suffering

we
are
all
dying

still—
we
could
go on
hugging
our
children
and
smiling
for
no particular
reason

we
could
take pleasure
in the first
snowy
day
of
winter

we
could
make
dinner
for
everyone
even when
that
sad
discontented
voice
inside
our
heads
relentlessly
asks,
"why
is
this
happening
to me?"
as though
no creature
other than
us
has
ever
suffered
illness
or
misfortune.

we
could
stop
waiting
for
life
and
live
without
expectations
and
find
ourselves—
at least
sometimes—
pleasantly
surprised
at
the
turn
of
events.

we
could
imagine
the
future
and
take

pleasure
in
all the
good
things
that
will
come
to
pass—
even
without
us.

we
could
be
content
with
here
and
now.

fears

fears
dancing
around
in
my
heart,
holding
me
back
from
embracing
my
wonderful
life
here
and
now.

Sunday
August 19, 2012

precipice

standing
at
the edge
of
a
precipice,
peering
down

a dark cavern

for now,
I
reside
in
a
dark
cavern—
crestfallen
and
forlorn

Friday
March 26, 2010
Piedmont, Ca

despair

I am
keeping
my
despair
to
myself

I
do not
want
to
hear
the
strident
voice
of
almost
anyone—
good naturedly
coaxing
me
towards
hope
and
love.

hope

hope
has
deserted
me.

I
am
worn
deadened
fossilized.

I
seek it
beseech it
beg of it
to return

"my heart,"
I say
"is
lost
and
forlorn."

yet
hope
does not
return
and

I
pretend to live—
my
habits
mapping
the day
ahead.

love

love
has
deserted
me.

I am
worn
deadened
fossilized.

I
seek it
beseech it
beg of it
to return

"my heart,"
I say
"is
lost
and
forlorn."

yet
love
does not
return
and
I

pretend to live—
my habits
mapping
the day
ahead.

                    Friday, March 26 2010
                    Oakland, Ca

Oakland Airport

sitting
at
the
gate
in
an
airport,
your
belongings
next
to
you,
your
unhappiness
as if
neatly
packed
somewhere
inside,
you
can
become
peacefully
resigned
and
content.

Sunday
March 28, 2010

1945 LNCO

what is
there
in the
emptiness
of
a
room
full
of
chairs
in
the
buzzing
sound
of
the
heater
and
my
lone
presence
that
comforts
and
soothes?

Monday March 1, 2010
University of Utah
Salt Lake City, Utah

untitled 1

"I
will
one day
burst
on
the
stage
of
life
and,
finally,
live."

Monday
April 5, 2010
Salt Lake City, Utah

untitled 2

your spirit
came
and
stood by
my
bed
as
I
lay
there.

I
sensed
you
felt
you
and
loved
you.

Friday
May 7, 2010
Piedmont, Ca

love and starbucks

love
demeaned

connected
to
starbucks
frappuccinos
banks
insurance companies
cell phones

love
demeaned

Monday
May 17, 2010
Piedmont, Ca

number 2 pencil

I
reside
in
the
happy
meeting place
of
a
number 2
pencil
and
white
paper.

March 16, 2011
Piedmont, Ca

enemies

sometimes
the
most
meaningful
relations
are
the ones
with
enemies.

Saturday
January 8, 2011
Piedmont, Ca

earth

the air
that we breathe

the water
that we drink

the rain
that falls on our heads

the wind
that brushes against our cheeks

have we
contaminated
and
polluted
all
these
elements?

ruin
and
destruction

shame
and
utter sadness

you are not alone

you are not alone
when your hand reaches
for the blue pen
and you softly write
on green colored
sheets of paper.

October 15, 1996
(Salt Lake City)

gratitude 1

a man
yelling
into
his
cell phone
while
crossing
the Oakland Avenue
Bridge
right
in front of
my windows
as
I was writing
my
gratitude
list
for
the day.

red shoes

I am
going
to
buy
a
pair of
red shoes
to go
with
my
new
outlook
in life.

Thursday, June 2009
Piedmont, Ca

transparency

for some time
I kept hearing
the word
"transparency"
without knowing
exactly what it meant
and being scared
or ashamed
to admit
my ignorance.

I have
now
come
to understand
what it means
and
I
am convinced
it
is
a
good thing
for both
institutions
and
our souls.

Sunday, May 4, 2003
Salt Lake City, Utah

landscapes

there is
an ocean
a mountain
inside
of me

all
the
waves
and
drops of water
all the rocks
and pebbles
and
stones

the ocean
rises
and
the mountain
sits
still

Wednesday
May 7, 2003
Salt Lake City

angst

replace
your own
angst
with—
at least—
thoughts
of
compassion
for
other people's
suffering

don't
reside
in
it

still—

have
self compassion
too

hold
it
like
a
small
wounded

child
who needs
your
love

we
all
need
your
love.

old clothes

I
keep
two
of
my
old
pants
in
my
closet
and
every
once
in
a
while
I
look
at
them
and
wear
them
so
I
would not
forget
the
time

when
I
was
sick.

dreams and hopes

sitting
in
the
ruins
of
shattered
dreams
and
hopes—
crestfallen
and
forlorn

Sunday
November 17, 2013
Salt Lake City, UT

time

I
love
and
hate
time

I
can
nestle
in
its
folds—
half
an hour,
a whole
day,
weeks,
months,
or
even
years—
feeling
as
though
I
am
immersed
in

an
eternity

and
then
come
those
days
rushing
rushing
towards
me—
wanting
me
to
be
what
I
am
not—
efficient
and
highly
functional

and
I
go
from
task
to

task—
there,
yet
eyeing
the
time
when
I
will
again
be
immersed
in
an
eternity.

Sims and Beverly

if
I
were
not
timid
I
would
hold
Sims'
hand
and
dance.

I
would
then
motion
to
Beverly
to
join
us.

dancers
dancing
together

to
the
voice
of
Nusrat Fatih Ali Khan

spring, 2014

while
I
slept
the
two
trees
at
the
end
of
my
alley—
right
across
from
the
Catholic church—
grew.

green
buds
on
their
branches
before
they
turn
into
white

blossoms
whose
scent
tells
me
it is
spring,
once
again.

Saturday, March 29 2014
Salt Lake City, UT

suicide

you
had
friends
over
for
dinner
on
sunday
night
and
by
8:30
monday
morning
you
hanged
yourself
with
an
elegant
scarf
that
you
had designed.

in
the
garage
after

writing
a two page
note
and
arranging
the
manuscript
of
your last
work—
what
were
the
final
thoughts
that
crossed
your
beautiful
mind?

how
utterly
trapped
you
must have
felt—
as
you
contemplated
the

reality
of
35 years
in
prison
and
your family
losing
all
they had
to
help
you?

you
were
so
young—
only
19—
with
what
everyone
thought
was
a bright future
that
for
a
short
time

you
could not
see.

I
want
to
utter
their
names
in
remembrance
and
mourning—
L'Wren Scott
David Foster Wallace
Aaron Swartz
Madison Holleran.

Friday
April 11, 2014
Salt Lake City

health

I
am
postponing
my
enjoyment
of
life
until
I
get
a
clean
bill
of
health
and
a
lifetime guarantee
that
I
will
live
for—
give or take—
another
30
or

40
years
without
a
hitch.

Wednesday
June 4, 2014
Salt Lake City, Utah

Foothill Road

I
saw
the
blocks
on
the
road
and
I was afraid.

I was afraid
of
hitting
them
and
falling
and
not
having
the courage
to
get
up.

silence

a
dark
chamber

unseeing
unknowing

silence

comfort
and
ease

Friday
June 27, 2014
Salt Lake City, UT

department meeting

marking
the
hours
and
minutes

the
sound
of
a
clock
on
the
wall

a
bare
room

chairs

everyone
quiet
and
alone
with

their
happiness
and
unhappiness

Friday
July 11, 2014
Salt Lake City

cliff

where
do
you
reside
in
the
course
of
the
day?

in
the
world—
out
there?

or
in
charted
habits?

or
somewhere
deep inside—
sitting
on

a
waterworn
cliff,
looking?

Gaza 2014

everywhere
I
look
I
see
flags
of
Palestine

Friday
July 25, 2014
Salt Lake City, UT

gratitude 2

gratitude
has
no
borders

it
deepens
and
deepens
till
the
end.

Friday
August 29, 2014
Salt Lake City, UT

joy

I
look
in
the
mirror
and
I
rejoice—
after
years
of
self doubt
and
uncertainty.

Saturday
August 30, 2014
Salt Lake City, UT

night

night
draws
near

doubt
fear
unease
descend
into
my
heart

I
watch
their
nightly
dance
and
when
morning
comes
I
see
them
depart.

Friday
September 12, 2014
Salt Lake City

hesitations

I
do not
want
to
hesitate
in
loving
people
anymore.

Saturday
February 7, 2015
Salt Lake City

Pia Farrenkopf

Pia Farrenkopf
sat
mummified
in
the
back
seat
of
her
car
for
5 years
before
anyone
noticed
she
was
dead.

she
kept
to
herself,
said
neighbors
and
sisters.

she
paid
her
bills
even
after
death
until
her
bank account
dried up.

it
looks
as if
one
evening—
fed up,
just fed up—
she
went
into
the
back
seat
of
her
car
in
the
garage

with
a
bottle
of
red wine
and
sat
there
and
waited
to
die.

my mother's advice

for many
years
I
did not
want
to
listen
to
my mother's advice—
big
or
small.

I
asked
her
about
a
purple
shirt
the other
day
and
this time
I
listened.

she
was
right.

Saturday
May 9, 2015
SLC, UT

Alfred Postell

Alfred Postell
went
to
harvard law school
and
graduated
in
the same year—1979—
as
the judge
who presided
over
his sentencing.

Alfred Postell
became
a
tax lawyer
with
a
firm
until
some time
in the mid 80s
when
he
bugged out
lost
all

that
he
had
and
started
wandering
the
streets—
hanging out
in front
of stores
and
in McDonald's

the
judge
remembered
him
from
law school
days
as
"extremely disciplined
a
very very
bright and
charming man."

Alfred Postell
remembered
his own past life—

"you get into a firm
it's prestigious,
and when you lose that position
it's like suicide.
or as accountants say
it's to be obsolete,
beyond your useful life.
I was beyond my useful life."

saffron chicken

the
Gods
are
watching
as
I
pour
salt
pepper
garlic
saffron
and
lemon juice
over
the
chicken pieces
and
cut up
onions
for
tonight's
dinner.

to Mushira

the aspens

I
believe
in
trees

their
leaves
and
branches
rustling
in
the
wind
their
tall
stature
and
bright
greens
shining
against
the
blue sky

a willing soul

today
my surgeon
Dr. Sharp
called
me
"a willing soul"—
something
I
want
to be
for
the
remainder
of
my
life.

Wednesday
April 27, 2016
Salt Lake City, UT

enemies 2

there
is
not
much
joy
in
seeing
the
defeat
of
enemies.

time
vanquishes
us
all.

Harry Sloan

Harry kissed my hand today
he leaned forward
looked at me
from head to toe
saying,
how elegant and beautiful I looked
how everything matched—
my shoes, my suit—
and as he led me out of the elevator
on the 7th floor of the Charleston Apartments
he kissed my hand.

Harry Sloan

Harry is eighty-some years old
and I am a thirty-something
single woman.
Harry lives in my building
and I am his friend,
he says.
his face lights up,
his blurry blue-gray eyes
as I approach and say,
"hi Harry."

he tells me stories
of his trip back East
and the service he got
on Delta

because of his cane,
his brown cane.

he tells me stories
of when he lived in Washington
thirty, forty some years ago
Massachusetts Avenue
American University
we both went there

he remembers
and
I listen.

one day
when Sharon said,
"I see Harry
you've got yourself a girlfriend,"
Harry said,
"she stimulates
my heart."

Harry Sloan

he kissed my hand today.

May 31, 1996
Salt Lake City, Utah

death

death
entered
rudely
unceremoniously—
before
she
had
a
chance
to finish
her
thought

they
left
together
hand in hand
and
others
sat
or
stood—
unknowing,
full

of
fright,
and
alone.

Tuesday, May 10, 2016
Salt Lake City, Utah

suicide, again

was
it
the
undignified
disease
that
assailed
him
in
the
last
few years?

(he
could
hardly
recognize
himself,
his
life)

when
was
that
day
that
moment
when
the pain

and
the agony
and
the indignity
became
unbearable?

he
climbed
up
a mountain hill
and
threw
himself
down
a cavern.

he
ended
it.

Thursday, May 21, 2016
Salt Lake City, Utah

1300 East

I
still
walk
the same
streets
I
used to
walk
20
years
ago
in
Salt Lake City.

I
see
the
same
trees
and
flower bushes
and
the
same
patch
of
grass
where
I

found
my
mother
and
sister
sitting
and
playing
with Sarah
one
summer
afternoon
when
I
was returning
home
from
my office.

my
heart
leaps
just
the
same
at
the
sight
of
the
pink

orange
yellow
and
lavender
colored
roses
in
the
front yard
of
a
house
close
to
the
Charleston apartments.

and
I
know
just
as
I
did
all
those
years
ago
that
I
will smell

the
roses
as
I
pass
the
front yard
on
my way
to
the
Charleston apartments.

Sarah Wisely

Sarah Wisely
is
a
twenty two
year old
woman
from
Pennsylvania
who
has
serious septic illness.

last year
she
had
her
twenty-second
round
of
infections
in
three years.

her doctors—
even
her favorite ones—
have asked
her
whether

she
is
ready
for
hospice care,
tired
simply tired
of
fighting.

she
has said
no
she
wants
to go on
living
she
wants
to
win.

she
has
many
wounds
on
her body
from
all
the

surgeries
she
has had.

she
is not
ashamed
of
her
scars
and
would
even
bare
them
if
asked.

"they
are
my
ups
and
downs.
my
weaknesses
and
my
strengths.
if
I

can feel
beautiful
in my
skin
why
shouldn't
everyone else?"

*(in appreciation of her insights
on jealousy and woundedness)*

to Anne Lamott

children
leave
or
bond
more
closely
with
their
dad.

parents
pay
more
attention
to
the
child
who
needs
them
more.

sisters
prefer
one another

to
you.

in
the
end—
or
what
feels
like
the
end
since
you
are
old—
you
know
that
you
have
to
let
go
of
the
woundedness
the
brokenness—
even though

at times
you
just
can't.

you
try
to
remember—
when
a
wonderful
emptiness
fills
your
soul—
the
words
of
the
mystics
who
say
our hearts
have
to be broken
to
let in
the
light.

old professor

there
is
something
sad—
almost pitiable—
in
seeing
an old professor
who
has long
retired
roaming
the
buildings
where
he
once
taught
on
campus

no longer
dressed
in
smart looking jackets
and
walking

with
a
spritely
gait

now

all shrunken
and
stooped
in
loose fitting clothes
and
walking
with
feeble
and
tired
steps

place

this
is
my
place
in
the
world—
the
little
corner
where
I
hear
the
breeze
passing
through
the
aspens
outside
my
window
late
at
night
or
in
the
course

of
the
day—
grateful
for
the beginning
of
autumn,
another
season.

this
is
my
place
in
the
world
where
I
retreat
from
all
the
noise—
sometimes,
cloistered
inside
myself.

Gwyndelyn Johnson

Gwyndelyn Johnson
from
Bowling Green, Kentucky
was
found
dead
in
her
bed
five months
after
she
died.

electricity
was
cut
off
to
her house
and
her
two
cars
were unmoved.

but
it
was
only
when
mail
piled up
in
her
front yard
that
neighbors
called
the police.

the
police
guessed
she
must have
been
dead
somewhere
between
five to six
months
and
one
police officer
remarked,
"sometimes

death
has
no
dignity.”

when no one looks for you

the
skeleton
of
a
man
who
might have
mistakenly
locked
himself
in
a
holding cell
at
an
abandoned
police station
was
found
in
Paterson
New Jersey
after—
most likely—
10 years.

a
bottled water
and

a
prescription drug
from
10
years
ago
right
next
to
his
decomposed
body.

short excursions

I
love
these
short
excursions
into
fantasy—
right
in the middle
of
the
day
and
amidst
tasks
and
obligations
and
responsibilities

watching
my
favorite
scene
of
a romantic movie
and
seeing
the gaze

of
love
between
soon-to-be
lovers
and
partners
in
life

Daniel von Bargen

Daniel von Bargen
tried
to
kill
himself
a
day
before
he
was scheduled
for
yet
another
amputation—
this
time
a few
toes—
because
of
diabetes.

he
told
the
911
dispatcher
who
answered

the
call
he
made,
"I
have
no
children
and
no
life.
I
have
fucked
it
up."

he
died
a
few
years
later
of
complications
due
to
diabetes.

untitled 3

my
love
for
you
is
like
no
other
love
that
I
have
ever
known

it
pains
and
gladdens
at
the
same time
and
I
chase
after
it.

deep sadness

a
deep sadness
washed
over
me
as
I
woke up
this
morning
from
a
dream
about
the
past—
years
and
years
ago

the
remainder
of
the
day
spent
in
chasing

hopes—
including
the
thought
of
a
serene
and
timely
death—
some time
in
the
distant
future.

holy

on
the
way
to
being
holy

suddenly—
anger
and
fear

tears
and
laughter

oh
foolish
foolish
me

oh
foolish
foolish
me

untitled 4

there
is
an
unraveling
that
is
taking place—
a
coming apart
unlike
anything
I
have
ever
experienced
in
the
past

it
is
as if
I
do not
know
or
recognize
the person, the self, the consciousness,
the soul, the spirit, the "I"—

that
inhabits
this
body.

untitled 5

you
are
so
much
more
vast
than
my
worst
pain

your
beauty
comforts—
sorrowfully—
and
I
grow
still

inaction

I
wish
we
were
all
plagued
by
inaction
and
would
stop
all
the
damage
to
ourselves
others
and
the
whole
of
existence
by
running around
doing
doing
doing.

Ram Dass

lately
I
have
been
trying
to let go
of
my
own
dislikes—
people
places
moments

and yet

I
feel
the
very
deliciousness
of
bitter
and
unkind
thoughts and emotions

and yet

there
is
a
stirring
inside
that
seems
to be
nudging
me
towards
letting
go—

a
reminder
of
what
Ram Dass
says,
"everything
must
be
rerun
through
your
compassion
machine."

the lower self

the
lower self
likes
nothing
better
than
to
snare
us

I
fall
into
its
trap
and
almost
immediately
remorse
courses
through
my
whole
body
and
soul.

stranger

run run run
grey shirted stranger

my
gaze
behind
you—
a
good
day
ahead

ego

fragile
egos
are
just
as
harmful
as
huge
egos
to
oneself
and
others

you

you
have
never
left
me

I
am
the one
who
keeps
leaving
and
coming
back—
filled
with
light
and
both
happiness
and
sadness
the minute
I
cross
the

threshold
of
your
door

night

night
draws
near
and
with
it
doubts
and
fears
and
unease—

in
the
past
I
always
fled
when
they
came

tonight—
I
stay.

Nasser Safaei and Yosemite

Nasser Safaei
was
an
engineer
a
leftist
a
soldier.

he
fought
in the
Iran-Iraq
war.

at
some
point
in
the
1980s
or
early
1990s
he
came
to
the
U.S.

he
went
to
University of Michigan
lived
in
one
of the
student co-ops.

co-op
life
suited
him—
sharing
things
talking
left
politics—
just
as
he
had
in
Iran.

he
married
Janet
at

some
point.

they
adopted
a
daughter—
Hanieh—
from Iran.

he
left
his
job
at Ford
and
his
physician wife
got
a job
in
New Mexico
and
they
all
settled
into
a
life
in
Albuquerque—

Nasser
beekeeping
building
a tree house
for Hanieh.

Nasser Safaei
died
unexpectedly
at
the age
of
47
in New Mexico
and
they
sent
his body
back to
Mashhad
where
he
was born.

I
remember
Nasser
telling
me
about
his

trip
to
Yosemite
when
we
were
all
students
at
Michigan
in
the
90s.

he
loved
it
found
it wondrous.

I
had
never
been
until
this
April.

and
the whole
time

I
was
in the park
I
saw
every
waterfall
rock formation
and
the
trees
and
meadows
as if
Nasser
was
there.

his
spirit—
eager
nature loving
kind
giving—
and
his
expansive
smile
all
in
Yosemite.

Jamba Juice

sitting
on
the
stone bench
in
front
of
Jamba Juice
in
Emeryville

the
warmth
of
the
sun
the
cool
bay breeze

a
bird's
nest
in
the
first
"a"
of
Jamba.

love and hesitation

there
is
something
old
and
worn
out
about
this
pain,
this
feeling
of
uncertainty
that
I
have been
carrying
around
since
childhood.

there
are
long
periods
when
it
feels

as
if
it
is
finally
gone.

then,
all of a sudden,
something
in
my
household—
a
conversation
where,
it seems,
I
am
not
included,
or
my
daughter
asking
for
my
husband
and
not
for

me—
brings
it
back.

and
as old as
I
am,
I
become
hesitant
in
my
love
and
do
not
want
to
let
go
of
the
familiar
pain

and
uncertainty,
even though
I
know
I
should.

here and now

my
soul
travels
to
far away
places
on
earth
and
times
in
the
past
and
comes
back.

I
am
happily
renewed
and
can
stay
right
here
and
now.

suicides

2206, 509 Madison Avenue, 2008

bottles
of
sleeping pills
near
his
desk—
he
locked
himself
in
his
office
and
slashed
his
left
arm—
close
to
a
wastebasket
so
there
would not
be

too
much
of
a mess.

Blaubeuren, 2009

walking
into
the
cold
on
Monday
night
in
Blaubeuren,
he
ran
in
front
of
a
train.

158, Mercer Street, SoHo, 2010

early
morning
hour—
he
hanged

himself
with
the
dog's
leash.

Sofitel New York Hotel, 2017

"I
feel
great,"
he
told
the
nanny
in
the
morning

in
the
afternoon
he
went
to
the
Sofitel New York Hotel,
jumped
from
his room
on

the
24th floor,
and
landed
on
the
balcony
of
one
of
the
rooms
on
the 4th
floor.

"I
feel
great,"
he
told
the
nanny
in
the
morning.

the road—away and home

the
road
away
from
home
is
steep
and
hard
and
I
hesitate
every
once
in
a while
and
wonder
if
I
can
go on.

but
I
go on
and
"keep
right on
till
the
end."

the
road
home
is
pleasant
and
I
hear
a
mild
breeze
passing
through
flowers
and
leaves
and
gently
stroking
my
face.

I
do
not
waver
in
my
resolve
and
I
come
to
my
favorite
bend
in
the
road
and
look
at
the
familiar
trees
and
flowers
and
raise
my
hand
in
thanks

to
a
man
who
lets
me
cross
the street.

now
closer
and
closer —
only
the
back
alley,
passing
in
front
of
the
two
churches,
a
row
of
white
garages
on

the
left.

then,
home.

Maryam Mirzakhani (1977-2017)

yesterday,
your
passing—
the
sorrow
of
sorrows.

Raashanai Coley

Raashanai Coley
died
of
an
infection
after
her
mother
punched
her
so hard
in
the
stomach
that
it
ruptured.

the
11 year old
girl
was
covered
in
cigarette
burns
and
scars.

Raashanai
spent
nights
in
a
closet
without
a
bed
and
ate
only
a
bowl
of
cereal
every day.

she
weighed
just
sixty seven
pounds
when
she
died.

the
mother
is
now

serving
time
in
jail
and
will be
there
for
many
years
to come.

at
her
hearing
the
judge –
aghast
and
in
disbelief –
cried out,
"how
can
humans
do
this?"

Wednesday
January 18, 2017

a grand affair

my
fears
dress up
in
evening gowns
and
invite
me
to
attend
a
grand
affair.

I
thank
them
and
politely
decline.

Wednesday January 18,
2017
SLC

dying in Arizona

Alan
was
a
gregarious
man.

he
knew
a lot
about
technology
despite
not being
that
young.

he
taught
at
university
for
many
years
and
then
at
some point
had
heart trouble

and
surgery.

so
along
with
his
professor
wife –
his love
and
companion
of
many years –
he
decided
it
was
time
to
retire.

they
would
travel
during
Christmas
and
summer –
going
to

Europe,
especially Hungary,
where
his wife
had been
born.

they
would
go
to
Hawaii
and
through
the years
took
many
cruises.

he
loved
good
food
and
good
company
and
kept up
with
politics
in

the
U.S.
and
abroad.

and
then
came
his
wife's turn
to
retire
and
he
persuaded
her
that
they
should move
to
a
retirement community
in
Arizona –
a place
full of
academics
just like
them.

she

was not
too
keen
on
the
idea
but
said
yes
and
there
they
went.

and
in
less
than
a
year
and
before
they
could
really
settle
into
this
new life
and
new home

and
new surroundings
they
found out
he
had
leukemia.

he
died
in
a
short
three months –
no
remaining
white blood cells,
said
the
doctors.

just
like
that –
as though
he
had gone
to
Arizona
to
die.

enemies, a story

I
never
knew
why
you
did not
like
me
these
twenty odd
years.

perhaps
at
some
point
the
dislike
went
away.

you
are
now
retiring
after
many
years.

in
the
last
few
meetings
when
my
glance
would fall
on
your face,
sitting
as
you
always
did
on
the
other side
of
the
rectangle
table,
I
thought
you
looked
frail –
old –
as
I

do,
as much as
I
hate
to
admit
it.

I
did not
sign
the
card –
wishing
you
much
joy and happiness
in
your
golden years.
I
did not
go
to
your
retirement
party.

I
felt
or

at least
told
myself
I
did not
want
to
be
a
hypocrite.

I
wish
you
well –
from
afar.

spirits

your
spirit
brushes up
against
thousands
of
other
spirits —
sometimes,
softly,
and
at other times,
in
confusion
and
with
a myriad
of
emotions
that
make
you
recoil
and
draw back.

enemies and time

is
it
possible
to
miss
enemies –
those
who
harmed
you
in
the
past
but
now
are
gone –
time
taking away
the
rancor
which
sat
in
your heart
for
so
long?

A Mennonite in Khiva is Soheila Amirsoleimani's
fifth collection of poetry. She lives in Salt Lake City
with her husband and daughter. She teaches in the
Department of World Languages & Cultures at The
University of Utah.